GEORGE MARTIN

A BIOGRAPHICAL SKETCH

ROBERT L. MARTIN

FOREWORD BY RICHARD D. WOLFF

ROBERT L. MARTIN
ANNANDALE-ON-HUDSON, NEW YORK

Copyright © 2016 by Robert L. Martin.

All rights reserved. No part of this publication may be reproduced, distributed or transmitted in any form or by any means, including photocopying, recording, or other electronic or mechanical methods, without the prior written permission of the publisher, except in the case of brief quotations embodied in critical reviews and certain other noncommercial uses permitted by copyright law.

Robert L. Martin
14 Faculty Circle, Bard College
Annandale-on-Hudson, New York 12504

Book Layout ©2013 BookDesignTemplates.com

George Martin: A Biographical Sketch / Robert L. Martin.
First edition.
ISBN 978-0-9974216-2-0

Contents

Foreword vii

Acknowledgements ix

Introduction 1

1904–1923: Sosnowitz, Poland 5

1923–1933: New York and California 13

1933–1945: New York, Syracuse, Philadelphia, Ohio, Washington DC 19

1946–1949: Portsmouth, Ohio 27

1949–1972: Cincinnati 43

Concluding Comment 51

Appendix 1: A Visit To Sosnowiec (2008) 55

Appendix 2: "Strike, 1949"—College Paper on the 1949 Selby Strike, by Robert Martin (1958) 61

Appendix 3: A Partial Family Genealogy 82

Appendix 4: A Retrospective on the "Communist-Dominated" Unions 85

*To my brother Gene,
and to the memory of our mother,
Sylvia Martin*

Foreword

AS THIS BOOK SHOWS, George Martin's life and work speaks to a central issue of his time but also of ours. Does the actual record of left-wing labor leaders, Communists, and their allies in the CIO reveal a betrayal of labor's interests for some "external" political goals? The book's chronicle of the life of one such ally and the well-chosen short final appendix answer this question with a resounding "no." Recent scholarship likewise supports that no.

Quite the contrary, the right-wing labor leaders (as well as the left-wing leaders who betrayed their former allies to avoid expulsion from the CIO) produced generally poorer contracts, wages, and working conditions for their members. The militance of unionists mattered then as it usually does.

George Martin's life is quietly told in this book, which is all the more moving because of the intimacy of its tone. It testifies to what is lost for the union movement and for the progressive left of politics when anti-communism is used to repress and exclude militants. The period of such repression and exclusion after World War II marked the start and enabled the continuation of that momentous long decline of the left and organized labor in the US that has shaped the world ever since. That decline allowed the US to play world capitalism's policeman as no other country could. It enabled the rise of neoliberalism and its accompaniment of income and wealth inequality of epic proportions. It invited the outright purchase of parties and politicians by super-rich individuals and corporations—a process that is now nearly complete.

This book documents nothing less than a micro-level look into the reality of how anti-communist repression and exclusion worked in and on one militant's life. What this book teaches is the terrible mistake working people and their leaders made (and what a price the world has paid) when so many of them knuckled under to anti-communism. The latter was little more than capitalism's tactic of the moment to destroy its opposition from below, the opposition of the majority to the injustices imposed by the minority.

Richard D. Wolff

Professor of Economics Emeritus, University of Massachusetts, Amherst
Visiting Professor, Graduate Program in International Affairs, New School University

Acknowledgements

MANY FAMILY MEMBERS READ early drafts and contributed helpful information and memories: my brother Gene, his wife Bette, and my cousins Carla Horowitz, Loren Bloom, and Judy Weisberger. I'm grateful to my friend Harvey Sperry for helping me realize that my father's story can have resonance and importance even for those who are not members of our family. My colleague John Halle did me the great favor of putting me in touch with the economist and historian Richard Wolff, to whom I am deeply grateful for providing a foreword to explain the broader social historical context of my father's life and work. I owe thanks to our son Jeremy for his help throughout the project, specifically for the laborious character-recognition scanning of my college paper and for the excellent idea of asking our friend Isabella Furth, director of Bluefish Editorial Services, to take on the task of editing the manuscript and bringing it to publication. Most of all, I am grateful to Katherine for the work she did on our family genealogy long before I started this project, and for her deep and sympathetic interest in my father's family. Beyond that, it is of course the fact that we made a family together that provided the children and grandchildren for whom I wrote. My gratitude for that knows no bounds.

Introduction

MY FATHER, GEORGE MARTIN, was quite a wonderful man. He was fun to be with: outgoing, quick witted, generous, warm, and thoughtful. He was a source of inspiration: idealistic but also pragmatic, and dedicated for his whole life to the improvement of the living conditions of men and women who work at factory jobs. He was a loving and devoted father and husband.

For many years, since his death in 1972, I've wanted to write an account of George Martin's life especially so that my children could know about him. Katherine's and my oldest son, Jeremy, came with me from Taiwan to the memorial service in 1972 but he was only four years old and had spent very little time with his grandfather. My brother Gene's children, Seth and Eric, did know George Martin and were deeply attached to him even though they were only ten and eight years old when he died. Two of George Martin's descendants were named for him—Seth's son George and my second son Benjamin George. Especially, then, for all of Gene's and my children and for our grandchildren, I want to write about George Martin's life.

It has taken a long time and been very difficult for me to write even this relatively brief account. The main difficulty has been my lack of knowledge—the puzzling truth is that I know very little about my father. Although he was in many ways a very nostalgic person, he didn't talk much about his past. He was nostalgic about events involving our family, almost before they happened, but he didn't speak about his life growing up in Poland or his years in the United States before meeting my mother. I wish I had asked more questions. The other challenge has been my incomplete knowledge of the history of organized labor in the United States. My father was deeply involved in his work, so the story of his life should include an account of the unfolding events of the labor movement. I've done the best I can.

In any case, it's time to begin. Here is the outline:

George Martin was born on January 7, 1904 in Sosnowitz, Poland, with the name Moszek (or in Yiddish, Moishe) Gottfried, the seventh of nine children in an orthodox Jewish family. He came to the United States at the age of 19, in 1923, by this time a non-believer and aligned with the left-wing politics associated with the "Bund" labor movement in Poland. He owed his chance to come to the United States to two of his older sisters and his brother-in-law, and after his arrival he spent his early time in Brooklyn working in a shoe factory. He traveled to the West Coast around the time of the Great Depression in 1929, and stayed there until around 1933, probably associated with the Young Pioneers movement of the American Communist Party. He returned to the East Coast in 1933 and met my mother, Sylvia Bloom, in 1934. My brother Eugene was born in 1936, and I was born in 1940. George worked first for the Boot and Shoe Workers of the American Federation of Labor (AFL) and then, from about 1934, for the United Shoe Workers of America of the Congress of Industrial Organizations (CIO), working throughout the Midwest and upper Midwest. In 1952 he was a victim of the McCarthy era purge of left-wing organizers from the US labor movement and his career as a union organizer ended. He and his family were living in Cincinnati, where he managed to find a series of office jobs. He devoted his energies to local Cincinnati Democratic politics and to his family. He died on November 3, 1972, at the age of 68.

Now I'll try to fill in some details, based partly on materials from his files and partly on my own recollections and those of Gene. Along the way I'll talk about aspects of the outside world that I think are important in understanding what a gifted and dedicated and heroic man my father was.

—January, 2014

[1]

1904–1923: Sosnowitz, Poland

Moishe Gottfried

SOSNOWIEC IS A SMALL city in the south of Poland, a short distance northeast of the larger city of Katowice and about one hour west of Krakow. "Sosnowiec" is the Polish name of the city; I always heard it referred to as "Sosnowitz," the Yiddish form of the name. My wife Katherine and I visited Sosnowitz in February 2008 with a guide from Krakow, a historian specializing in Jewish history who was then the head of research at the Auschwitz Jewish Center. My hope was to see the street and the house where my father grew up but we had no address, and when we did eventually get his birth certificate it contained no home address for his parents. Our guide identified the pre-World War II Jewish section of Sosnowitz, principally one long street, Modrzejowska, and two side streets, Kolejowa and Targowa. We walked along these streets, peering into the courtyards and in the windows of the apartments, trying to imagine my father living there as a boy. (I've included my 2008 account of our visit to Sosnowitz as Appendix I at the end of this account.)

Figure 1: Sarah Tendler and Abraham Gottfried 1918

My father's parents were Abraham Gottfried and Sarah Tendler. I grew up hearing that my grandfather Abraham was a rabbi, so I imagined him in a temple, but I learned later that the title signified only that he was a religious man who spent most of his time studying and praying and had no other occupation. Family lore had it that my grandmother Sarah cooked Shabbat and Pesach meals for Jewish inmates of the local jail; I also heard that she and my grandfather managed an inn, though I suppose it is more likely that they simply took in Jewish travelers who wouldn't have been accepted at local hotels or inns. I know that they had many children—my father was the seventh—and many came after him. I know that Abraham was blind. Abraham and Sarah died in the Holocaust, sometime between September 1939, when the Germans entered Sosnowitz, and 1944. Three of their children—Manya, Dora, and my father—had settled in the United States by then. A few others survived the war: One daughter settled later in Israel, and one son (Chuna) settled in Argentina.

(Dora's daughter Judy told me that Dora and Manya were told after the war that Abraham and Sarah died at home.)

My father spoke very little of his childhood. I recall only three things he described, and my memory of them is so hazy as to suggest that I heard them when I was very young. In one, he described sitting at the dining room table and hiding cooked potatoes in a little drawer near his seat, because the family ate potatoes at almost every meal and he was sick of eating them. He told me that the potatoes were discovered when they became rotten and smelled.

Figure 2: Moishe Gottfried front and center

Another story was that he was chosen by his father to lead him around when he went out, and to spend hours with him, joining him in the chanting and singing of prayers. My father told me that at some point (perhaps at the age of about 14) he had the courage to ask his father why he needed to keep his eyes closed during prayers, and was told that he would be struck dead if he did not. The story ended, of course, with my father fearfully opening his eyes during a prayer, surviving, and becoming an atheist. There is no doubt about the last part of the story—he was an unswerving atheist for his entire adult life. There was never a sign that he was sentimental or nostalgic for the religious life of his upbringing. Gene recollects that Dad argued with his father about religion, until his father angrily and plaintively said that he believed that God took away his sight to purify him in some fashion and thereby gave him something of value—"why," he asked Moishe, "would you take that away from me?" Gene isn't sure about the story of Dad's opening his eyes during a prayer, but he remembers the story that the first time Dad found himself really doubting the existence of God he expected to be struck dead.

The third thing I associate with my father's years in Poland is an image of a particular way that young men dressed—with a white shirt open at the collar, with the collar spread over the lapels of a suit jacket. I imagine him dressed that way, listening to music at a concert, or engaged in a political or historical discussion. It stood in contrast to the picture of the religious Jew engaged in prayer, dressed in black with yarmulke, earlocks, prayer shawl, etc.

Gene's understanding is that when Dad was young he started spending time with leftist University students, who adopted him as a "mascot." On one occasion they took him to a concert. He had a nice coat but his pants had a hole in them. Afterwards his friends invited him to a party, which he was delighted to attend. Once there, his friends kept saying "Take off your coat and stay." He said no (because of the hole in his pants) but he stayed with his coat on. Later a girl asked him what really happened. He explained—she insisted that he take off his pants and give them to her to mend, which he did (and she did).

Political Awakening

To understand how Dad may have moved from the world-view of the orthodox Jew to the political beliefs that shaped the rest of his life, it is important to consider the period around 1920 in Poland when he was 16 years old. At this time the "Bund"—a Jewish socialist party that promoted the political and social well-being of Jewish workers—was active in Poland. The Polish Bund was an outgrowth of "The General Union of Jewish Workers in Lithuania, Poland, and Russia,"[1] which was founded in 1897 by a small group of Jews who were influenced by Marxism and by the pervasive anti-Semitism around them and who sought to attract East European Jews to the then-developing Russian revolutionary movement. Working-class Jews, effectively barred from the more advanced industries, worked mostly in sweatshops under poor conditions and with low wages. The Bund was the result of interaction between these workers and a group of young Jewish intelligentsia (as they were called) who were attracted to various forms of Marxism and socialism. The Russian Bund's founders did not view their organization as specifically Jewish, and their ultimate aim was to integrate the Jewish worker into the general Russian proletariat. Lenin, though, saw the Bund as a national Jewish party with "dangerous" independent political tendencies and would later move to suppress it. When Poland fell under German occupation in 1914 an independent Polish Bund was established, and this group went on to sharpen its ideological positions after the war. It opposed Zionism, the movement that favored creation of a separate Jewish state in Palestine. The Bund viewed Zionism as based on an irresponsible illusion—that Jews could create a Jewish state like the one that existed 2,000 years earlier—and representing only the interests of bourgeois Jews. The Bund saw itself as the guardian of secular Yiddish Jewish culture, vigorously warding off attempts to cultivate Hebrew culture in Poland.

While it is not clear that my father was ever formally a member of the Polish Bund, the themes they upheld are those that I recognize from growing up with him: opposition to Zionism, and the belief that Jewish identity was secular, not religious, and linked to class struggle rather than to Hebrew culture. (Yiddish, not Hebrew, was my father's language.) Throughout his life, George Martin under-

---

[1]. My source is the *Yivo Encyclopedia of Jews in Eastern Europe*.

stood the term "left-wing politics" as commitment to social justice and to fighting against class prejudice and racism. This commitment was pragmatic, not doctrinaire, and he expressed it in actions rather than memberships or allegiances.

Figure 3: Passport photo, 1923

In 1923, Moishe—then nineteen years old—traveled via Belgium and the Netherlands to the United States. He received his visa at the American Consulate General in Warsaw on July 30, 1923, and entered the United States on September 2. His passport (issued the same year) listed his name as Moszek Gottfried, his profession as "living with parents (without profession)," his height as medium, his visage as oval, his hair as black, and his eyes as "beer colored" (in French: "chocolate"). His visa showed him to be going "To brother in US, Abram Hamburger, 267 West 143rd Street, New York City."

Moishe was able to come to the United States because of his two older sisters who had already emigrated. His sister Manya, his closest relative for the rest of his life, was fourteen years older. Manya had married Abram Hamburger at the age of nineteen and come to the United States in 1909, when Moishe was only five. Another sister, Deborah (Dora), four years older than Moishe, stayed in Sosnowitz until 1921, when Moishe was seventeen. It appears that Manya first arranged Dora's emigration to the United States, and then, two years later, brought Moishe. Two years later, in 1925, Sam Kokot came from Sosnowitz to New York; he and Dora were married in 1927.

[2]
1923–1933: New York and California

MOISHE LIVED WITH MANYA and Abram Hamburger in Brooklyn, New York. He worked in a shoe factory in Brooklyn as a "stitcher," sewing the tops on shoes. He became a shop steward, a union position, in the factory.

Figure 4: George in center

I associate this period of my father's life with his name change. He was always eager and enthusiastic, and he was given (or took) the name George from the expression, "Let George do it," applied to eager and enthusiastic people who step up when no one else will. I don't know how he came to have the name "Martin." It seems incredible to me now that I never asked him how he came to have the name George Martin. Gene recalls Dad telling him that he wanted a name that was not foreign-sounding. It seems clear that Dad came to the new world determined to have a new life and for that reason he chose a new name. It was only many years later, long after he died, when I met relatives with the name Gottfried, that it began to dawn on me that I too could have had the name Gottfried, and began to think about the significance of that long-ago name change.

The actual name change, to George Martin, came long after he had arrived in the United States. On February 7, 1936, exactly seven months before Gene was born, my father filed for naturalization in New York Eastern District and was still listed as Morris Gottfried of 2145 77th Street, Brooklyn, New York. He received the naturalization certificate on May 12, 1936. It seems natural to suppose that he wanted to become a US citizen before becoming a father. It's harder to imagine why it took him two more years to officially change his name, which he did on April 18, 1938, by decree of the City Court in Brooklyn. I have the impression that he called himself George long before 1938. My mother knew him from 1934, and seems always to have known him as George Martin.

My father traveled to the San Francisco Bay Area around 1929, and he stayed there until around 1933. During that time, he worked as a youth leader in the Young Pioneers movement. There are snapshots of him with groups of young people, but we really know nothing of why he travelled to the West and what he did. Gene recalls one of the few anecdotes that either of us knows from this period in Dad's life:

that in California on a sunny day he stripped to the waist—the European sun-lover—and ended up in the hospital with severe sunburn.

Figure 5: With the Young Pioneers

I assume that his activities at this time—1929 was the start of the Great Depression—had much to do with the American Communist party and the political activities of the American left. His sister Manya was a strong "left winger" and Dad was always involved, to a greater or lesser degree, with "the movement." I remember intense discussions in the circle of friends and relatives (including Manya's sons-in-law, both of whom fought in the Abraham Lincoln Brigade against fascism in the Spanish Civil War); in these discussions, Dad was always on the side of pragmatism against ideological "purity."

The decisive step in his career was his joining the labor movement—in particular the organizing of shoe workers—which seems to have occurred when he returned from the West Coast to New York in 1933. He had worked in a shoe factory when he first came to the United States a decade earlier, and I understand that he rose within the shoe factory in Brooklyn to become a shop steward. I know also that his older brother-in-law, Sam Kokot, was associated with the

Figure 6: "Study Group"

union—at that time the Boot and Shoe Workers' Union—so it's likely that Sam was involved in Dad's finding his way to that union.

I've often wondered why I knew so little about these matters—in particular, Dad's life before 1933, when he met my mother, Sylvia. I think there were at least two reasons. One is that Dad was married before he met her: he married Nadia (called Nelly) in San Francisco on December 10, 1929. She was seventeen; he was twenty-five. Nelly returned with him to New York in 1933. Mom knew Nelly and spoke of her easily and without hostility, but Dad may have felt it was wrong to talk with us about his life with a woman other than our mother. The second reason is that by the time Gene and I were old enough to learn about such things, the political climate in the United States, especially the fierce anti-Communist "red-baiting" of the cold war, made it seem dangerous to talk about—and for children, dangerous to ask about—activities of the earlier years. For whatever reason, we knew very little.

[3]

1933–1945: New York, Syracuse, Philadelphia, Ohio, Washington DC

The Birth of the CIO

FROM THIS POINT ON, Dad's story has to be told on two levels: in his work and with his family. For all the years of our childhood, his work was a "calling," not a job. It was something he did because he believed in it deeply. Only much later, in Cincinnati when he was forced from the union, did he have a job in the usual sense—something that one does to make a living. That contrast was very vivid and very painful for me. I remember when he went from being dedicated to his work—part of a cause, part of *the* cause—to having a variety of boring jobs that his friends helped him find when he was forced from the labor movement. He was disappointed but not bitter about it. That made a deep impression on me—it was as though he joined the ranks of the millions of working people who work at jobs of no particular interest in order to feed their families and send their kids to college. Because of the political swing of the country, he had lost the chance to earn a living doing what he cared about most. In fact the stigma of having worked as a union organizer left him unable to find many other kinds of employment. I have often felt how fortunate I have been to find employment doing what I love to do.

Figure 7: George Martin front and center with Union members in Portsmouth, Ohio

Dad came to his work as a union organizer at what must have been a tremendously exciting time for a young leftist idealist: the birth of the Congress of Industrial Organizations—the CIO. His work as a labor organizer began around the same time that the CIO broke away from the American Federation of Labor in 1936.

Until the creation of the CIO in 1936, the union movement had been dominated by the craft unions, which grew out of the guilds of medieval Europe. These were tightly controlled groups of skilled workers in particular fields—electricians, carpenters, dye makers, etc. The confederation of these craft unions known as the AFL—American Federation of Labor—was founded in the 1920s by Samuel Gompers. Within the ranks of the AFL there emerged a movement to break free of its earlier traditions and in particular to empower *industrial* unions, in which all workers in the same industry are organized into the same union regardless of differences in skill. This movement, led by John L. Lewis of the United Mine Workers, was resisted by the leadership of the AFL but finally emerged victorious.

People like George Martin, steeped from their early years in Europe in socialist and communist principles, must have been enormously excited to be part of a new union movement that would bring benefits to the masses of workers, not only protection to the skilled elites among them. During that decade and despite the effects of the Depression "the number of unionized employees tripled from 2,805,000 in 1933 to 8,410,000 in 1941....the proportion of workers enjoying union rights and protection jumped from 9 to 14 percent in manufacturing, 21 to 72 percent in mining, 23 to 48 percent in transportation, and 54 to 65 percent in construction. A new kind of workers' power had been mobilized in countless factories and communities. For the first time millions of industrial workers asserted rights that had to be respected, and created organizations that finally gave them some control over their world."[2]

Dad became a labor leader at a time when he was needed—he had the skills and dedication and energy to make a significant contribution to the development and the work of the trade union movement. The end of Dad's work in the trade union movement in 1952 coincided with the end of the CIO as a separate entity and its merger with the AFL.

The Family

Dad's first stint as a union organizer was with the Boot and Shoe Workers of the AFL, organizing shoe repairmen. He lived at 208 East 12th Street in New York City's Greenwich Village. In 1934, my mother, Sylvia Bloom, came to work at the union office. Dad ended his relationship with Nelly and began a new relationship with Mom.

---

2. James R. Green, *The World of the Worker: Labor in Twentieth Century America* (New York, 1980), pp. 172-3. For a clip about the birth struggle of the CIO, see http://www.youtube.com/watch?v=2IsJZAknuIQ.

Here is Gene's account of the way they met, which he got from Mom. Mom had been sent by her father, Isaac Bloom, to New York to chaperone her younger sister Clara, because Clara insisted on going to New York and was living with a young man (also from Springfield, Massachusetts) named Martin Bloom. (It was a coincidence that he had the same last name.) Sylvia was working in the "Free Tom Mooney" movement office in NYC. Sylvia met there a man named Sam Kokot, who told her about a job at the Shoeworkers Union. Sam Kokot, as I mentioned, was Dad's brother-in-law. Sylvia applied and got the job, collecting dues at the membership meetings. Apparently all the young women were talking about the new young organizer, George Martin. He came over to her and said "Do you like opera?" Their first date was at the opera.

Sylvia Bloom was born on March 10, 1911, in Lynn, Massachusetts. Her parents, Isaac and Betty Bloom, came from Riga (Latvia) and eventually settled in Springfield, Massachusetts, when Sylvia was quite young. Sylvia was an excellent student in an academically strong high school in Springfield and attended Worcester State Teachers College, where she was an English major, before going to work in New York City. She had a left wing (or as we called it, "progressive") upbringing. Her father, a man of very strong and very independent beliefs, was at various times a member of the Communist Party USA. From what I could gather he was a difficult and demanding father. My mother was devoted to him. Part of what attracted her to George Martin was the political perspective he shared with her father.

In 1935 Mom and Dad moved to Philadelphia. Sylvia was pregnant and miscarried. Gene understands that they were on relief at the time, and that the doctor accused her of aborting herself.

My parents did not officially marry at that time. They had arranged a very private ceremony, on a hilltop early one morning, to declare themselves committed to each other. It was a principled statement on their part—that marriage was a personal matter, not in need of sanction by the state—to marry this way. (However, Gene's recollection is of a different reason: that Dad wasn't then divorced from his previous wife.) In 1958, 24 years after they met, they did officially marry, in Fish Creek, Wisconsin, during a summer festival at which I had a job, in order to guarantee that their life insurance would devolve appropriately. They chose that place, far from where we lived in Cincinnati, Ohio, in order to avoid having friends and neighbors read about it in the court proceedings in the newspaper. It was quite exciting to be told, at age 18, that my parents had just gotten married!

On September 9, 1936, Gene (Eugene Victor Debs Martin) was born in Philadelphia. Money was tight. Gene recalls that when he was young he had pneumonia. The doctor wanted them to take Gene to the hospital, but partly because they couldn't afford the hospital they saw a different doctor who prescribed a new drug—sulfa. For some of the years after Gene's birth, our parents took in a boarder, a young

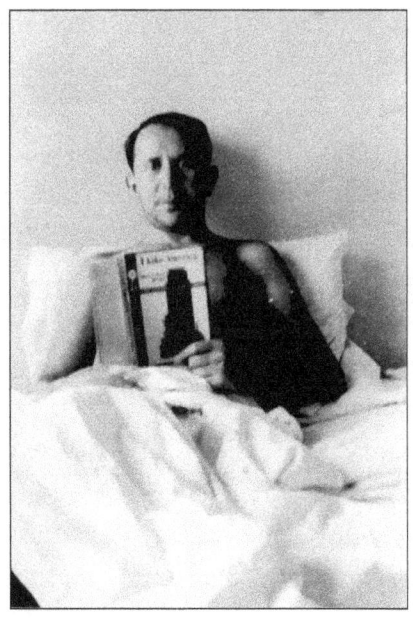

Figure 8: Reading *I Like America* by Granville Hicks, published 1938

music student named Russell Brodine, to help make ends meet. My parents had a strong effect on Russ, who later recalled teaching Gene, three years old, to bang on the table with his knife and say "I demand the salt." In the early months of 1940, though, my parents told Russ that he needed to move out because my mother was expecting a second child and there would be no room for a boarder in our apartment. I was born in March, 1940, in Philadelphia. Many years later, around 1958, I met a bass player from the St. Louis Symphony Orchestra named Russell Brodine. Russ was in the fact the student who had lived with my parents when he was a student at the Curtis Institute of Music, the school that I later attended. Russ had gone on to marry a union organizer, perhaps another testament to my parents' influence.

In 1941 our family moved from Philadelphia to Syracuse, where Dad was assigned to organize Nettleton Shoes. In the spring of 1942, the family moved to Norwood, a suburb of Cincinnati, where Dad was assigned to organize Red Cross Shoes. Gene recalls that we lived upstairs in a stucco building that had a porch off the living room. He remembers putting a pet worm on the porch but it shriveled up and died.

During the war years, George apparently made several attempts to join the army. On November 21, 1944, he was classified 4-A by the Selective Service, meaning that he was disqualified from the draft on account of his age.

After several months the family moved for the third time in two years—this time to Greenhills in Hamilton County, Ohio, one of three planned communities developed by the US government in the 1930s during the Great Depression. (The other two were Greenbelt, Maryland and Greendale, Wisconsin.) Gene remembers going into the woods looking for scrap metal to help with the war effort; he also remembers Roosevelt's death in May, 1945 and the shock of seeing adults cry.

During the war, my mother's sister Clara and her children Carla and Loren came to live with us while Clara's husband Martin Bloom served in the army. We stayed close to them throughout the years. In 2014, Carla recounted her memories of George in a letter:

> My clearest and fondest memories of George (besides always feeling how kind he was) are what a fabulous cook he was. To me the epitome of his artistry was his Matzo Brei.[3] Whenever we visited you in Cincinnati, Loren and I would drool with anticipation. One year I remember standing in the kitchen and writing down his recipe as well as his process so Mom could make it for us in Springfield. (I don't think she ever did.) I also remember a fabulous cake he made with balls of dough rolled in butter and cinnamon and sugar and walnuts—some kind of Hungarian babka??? Anyway, to this day Matzo Brei is still my favorite (soul) food. I try not to make it more than a few times a year due to the caloric content, but I ALWAYS think of George when I'm making it, and I know I have never been able to replicate the amazing taste he was able to create from this seemingly simple dish. And thanks to George's recipe, I was able to convert Milt, who grew up not liking Matzo Brei at all (his mother was not a good cook), to loving it.

STRUGGLES WITHIN THE CIO

The CIO, which had a national office in Washington DC, consisted of a large group of national affiliate unions, e.g., the United Mine Workers, the United Auto Workers, the United Steel Workers, and the United Shoe Workers. Each of these affiliate national unions had its own leadership and its own national conventions, and sent delegates to the CIO national convention as well. Each CIO-affiliate national union consisted in turn of local unions throughout the country—so, for example, there was Local 156 of the USWA–CIO (the United Shoe Workers of America–CIO) in Vanceburg, West Virginia, and Local 120 of the USWA–CIO in Portsmouth, Ohio. These locals

---

3. Matzo pan-fried with eggs.

were often grouped by state and held their own annual state-level conventions. Sometimes groups of these locals came together in District Councils. Dad held a position as organizer with the national affiliate union, the USWA–CIO: his title was Regional Director for Kentucky, West Virgina, and Ohio. He was also elected vice president of the Ohio chapter of the USWA–CIO, and at one point he was elected president of District Council No. 2 of the USWA–CIO, which included seven locals. These elected positions carried responsibilities but, I think, no salary. Dad's salary came from the national office of the United Shoe Workers of America–CIO.

In 1945 the family moved yet again, this time to Washington DC, where Dad was sent by the Union to edit the *Shoe Workers' Journal*. His transfer to Washington was apparently the result of an internal struggle in the national office of the CIO, in which the "traditional" unions, e.g. the Mine Workers, were gaining control over the left-wing industrial unions. The family lived at 2502 Alison Court, Apartment 3, Mount Rainer, Maryland, and Dad and Mom put a down-payment on a new house in Silver Spring, Maryland. But it turned out that Dad had been sent to Washington to remove him from a position of influence, and shortly after arriving there he was fired. When fired, George withdrew funds from the house.

At this seemingly hopeless juncture, the "rank and file" workers in the Portsmouth, Ohio union voted to have him return to Portsmouth as an organizer. I don't understand exactly how this turn of events came to be, but Dad's support from the workers in Portsmouth led to his reinstatement as an organizer for the USWA–CIO. At that point, Dad and Mom made a down-payment on a house in Portsmouth.

[4]

1946–1949: Portsmouth, Ohio

The Family

We moved to Portsmouth in 1946—actually the house was in Coles Park, Ohio, near Portsmouth. Coles Park consisted of three dirt roads perpendicular to Galena Pike. There were three cross streets. Most of the residents of Coles Park were sharecroppers who planted and harvested corn in the flood plain area near the Ohio River. According to Gene, only three houses (including ours) had indoor plumbing. Our closest neighbors, the Howards, had outdoor plumbing, though they were building a new house at the time.

This is the first place I remember very clearly. It seemed quite a fine house to me, with a living room, dining room, and large kitchen on the first floor and three bedrooms on the second floor, a garage with an attached room in the back, and a nice back yard. The house contrasted sharply with the Howards' quite dilapidated house, where I spent quite a bit of time playing. I have happy memories of our life there—I played in the hills and on the nearby farms, learned to swing on vines, and enjoyed school. Because of my age, I was shielded from the problems caused by Dad's work and the fact that he and Mom were apparently the only two who voted Democratic in the elections. Dad seemed happy, engaged, and confident. I remember the large drafting desk he set up in the living room where he laid out the union newspaper—the *Shoe Workers' Champion*—that he edited.

Gene describes a sense of living in a hostile environment in Portsmouth. He says that he felt he had no right to expect his parents to protect him—that such a feeling would be a betrayal of the "cause," so he suppressed his feelings of fear. He recalls a 7th grade field trip of our school, the Lower Dry Run School, to the Ohio State Penitentiary, which made a dark impression. He remembers that kids who played with him got in trouble. He says that his only friend was a boy whose drunken father abused his mother.

During our years in Portsmouth, Gene was in 5th, 6th, and 7th grades. I was in 1st, 2nd, and 3rd grades. There were, according to Gene, 7 rooms in the school and one for the furnace. Switches, for disciplinary purposes, were kept in the furnace room in a bucket of water so they would stay flexible—that I remember clearly. According to Gene, the only teacher with a college degree was the sixth grade teacher. Gene remembers the 5th grade teacher, Mrs. South, as very brutal and a frequent user of the paddle. Both of us remember the stern principal, Vernon McCall.

What Was Happening in the Labor Movement

The years of World War II, ending in 1945, had been a period of relative strength for the unions, in terms not only of improved working conditions but also of good relations with the government. The CIO strongly supported Roosevelt and the New Deal, even to the extent of agreeing to no-strike policies. In return, the unions enjoyed strong support from the Roosevelt administration. That administration created the National Labor Relations Board, which supervised and certified union elections, provided arbitration between unions and management, and, generally, validated the unions. The war ended with the United States in alliance with Great Britain and the Soviet Union as part of the so-called "Big Three" powers. This meant that CIO locals whose leaders were members of the CPUSA (Communist Party of the USA), or who were openly sympathetic to the policies advocated by the CPUSA, were able to function effectively within the CIO.

All that deteriorated rapidly in 1946 and 1947. There was a major post-war realignment of international politics in which US right-wing forces found political advantage in fostering a climate of anti-Communist fear and hysteria. In March of 1946, Walter Reuther was elected president of the powerful United Auto Workers on an anti-Communist platform. In May, 1946, the CIO established a "Committee for Renovative Trade Unionism," widely understood as aimed at combating Communism in the locals. (This focus on anti-Communism, associated with the activities in Washington of Senator Joseph McCarthy, was known as "red baiting" among left-wingers.) These developments were of course reflections of the beginning of the Cold War, which was to dominate US foreign policy for four decades. Henry Wallace, who had served as vice president under Roosevelt and was serving in the cabinet of President Harry Truman, spoke out in September of 1946 against Truman's 'get tough' policy toward the Soviets; Wallace supported a continuation of Roosevelt's policy of good relations with the Russians. In response, Truman dismissed Wallace from the cabinet, setting the stage for Wallace's decision to run for president against Truman as a 3rd party (Progressive) candidate. The CPUSA took a strong position in support of Wallace's 3rd party candidacy, exhorting the unions to support him also, even as the national CIO opposed his candidacy.

The *Shoe Workers' Champion*

One of Dad's main activities, starting in March, 1946, and continuing for at least three years, was to create and produce the *Shoe Workers' Champion*, a monthly newspaper for Ohio Valley District Council 2. The *Champion* was written, edited, and laid out in our living room in Coles Park. In it one hears Dad's "political" voice and sees the strategies he employed to build the morale and ethos of the local union. His people, the workers in the shoe factories in the three-state area, for the most part lacked college education; many had not even completed high school. A major focus of the *Champion* was education of all kinds, especially labor education, and pride-building. We see in the pages of the *Champion* the reversals in the trade union movement and the onset of the Cold War as gathering dark clouds, even as we read the *Champion*'s upbeat account of the day-to-day work of the union leaders and elected rank and file union members to improve working conditions in the shoe factories. One sees also reflections of Dad's personal struggle amidst the growing frenzy of anti-Communism within the labor movement, a struggle that eventually became a struggle for survival.

A one-year subscription to the monthly *Champion* cost $1. The paper consisted of news articles, editorials, signed columns, and photographs. There were advertisements from local businesses such as Henry Café ("Where the Shoe Workers Meet...Your Pay Checks Cashed Free"). There were articles on community activities such as picnics, sports events, and bowling leagues for children and adults, as well as news of illnesses, births, deaths, and social events. The first *Champion* editorial in the March 1946 issue was titled "Hi Ya, Folks," and began, "We were created to bring to you the latest news from each Local and from the District Council and to carry out any other tasks that you will assign to us from time to time." The editorial connected at once to the concerns of the individual locals:

- The strike of the H. C. Godman workers in Logan and Columbus and their courageous spirit of determination is something that we are all proud of...
- The splendid contract negotiated in Selby's is another orchid to our 117'ers...
- Our sisters and brothers of Vanceburg Local 156 and the Vulcan workers of Local 120 in Portsmouth are in the process of negotiation for their new contract...
- Brooks workers of Local 146 in Nelsonville will be host—for the first time—to the District Council...
- Although their contract does not expire until August 31st, Parkersburg Local 154 proudly boasts that the workers have received a 5% increase and expect shortly to add Hospitalization for all members...

This opening editorial set the tone for all subsequent issues of the *Champion*: proud, upbeat, and focused on the issues of importance to the workers.

George Martin's regular column "In Our Opinion (We Invite Yours)" began in the third issue, and by the fifth issue there were three additional signed columns by local union leaders, including one by a war veteran entitled "Tips for Vets." George Martin's first column went directly to national labor politics: "It was an evil day for the American people when the House of Representatives voted to smash price control (OPA) to pieces." He blasted the Ohio representatives McCowen and Brehm for their votes. Noting that the United States Senate "has within its power to reverse the House vote," he asked his readers to write to their senators right away and "be sure your neighbors and friends do the same." He linked the owner of the Shelby Shoe Company in Portsmouth to the move to eliminate price controls, and closed with a rhetorical flourish: "In the name of common sense we say, it is high time that management realizes that the spiral knife of inflation that first stabs the working people soon afterwards throws the entire economic machine out of order[,] bringing disaster and chaos to the entire population including even our well-provided-for management heads."

I will describe highlights of twelve issues, from March 1946 through February 1947. In addition to the organizing work being conducted in the locals, the issues chronicle escalating struggles between the left-leaning United Shoe Workers of America and its red-baiting president Frank McGrath. We know that in many cases the national office of the CIO tried to topple the avowedly Communist leaders of CIO affiliate unions (for example, Harry Gold of the Fur Workers, or Frank Bridges of the California Longshoremen's Union). But McGrath's case was especially extreme, as he joined the anti-Communist crusade and attempted to purge members of his own organizing staff. However, as we shall see, McGrath himself was finally voted out by his union and George Martin was able to continue his organizing work.

The very first issue of the *Champion*, from March, 1946, repudiated Frank McGrath for his red-baiting activities and called for his removal from office in the coming election. McGrath's office in Washington DC, was said to be responsible for re-election leaflets accusing officers of the District 2 local unions of attempting to "make the *Daily Worker* the United Shoe Workers' official journal and Communism the religion of all Shoe Workers." The *Champion* listed five indictments against McGrath, accusing him of actions injurious to the shoe workers. The third indictment described George Martin's transfer to Washington DC, and subsequent dismissal as an attempt to "deprive the Ohio Valley Shoe Workers of George Martin's tried, true and tested leadership." This indictment was accompanied by photostats of two letters from McGrath to George Martin. The first, dated May 29, 1945, set out Martin's responsibilities in a new assignment in Washington D.C., principally to produce a monthly newsletter and various pamphlets as requested by the Education Committee, and to serve as "legislative agent" for the national USWA–CIO. The second letter, dated November 13, 1945, informed Martin that his "services as a representative of the United Shoe Workers are discontinued." The *Champion* article offered no direct explanation for these actions but suggested that McGrath might be "in cahoots with sinister forces" to remove George Martin from the scene. "McGrath has no answers," the *Champion* asserted, "so he shouts 'Reds!...Commissars!'" Apparently, Dad's reassignment to Washington DC was meant to curtail his role as a powerful organizer in the field, in preparation for dismissing him altogether. The first issue of the *Champion* was a victory lap of sorts: five months after his attempted ouster, here Dad was, back in Portsmouth, working to build cohesion among the shoeworkers—and now denouncing the president of the national union.

The second issue of the *Champion* (April, 1946) records that McGrath was re-elected by 863 votes—and that election fraud was charged. The third issue (May, 1946) records that new elections were called for.

Meanwhile, we see in the *Champion* accounts of the organizing that went on during these contentious times. There was a report of evening classes throughout April, 1946, taught by George Martin, in which local officers and stewards could "learn latest methods of handling grievances and conducting local union affairs." The fourth issue (June, 1946) featured pictures of 16 smiling union members who attended the classes: "'It was a good start and we need lots more...' was the general opinion of all students." The sixth issue (August, 1946) included a signed article by an elected leader of one of the locals, praising the classes on collective bargaining, current legislation, political action, and education methods in local unions, "so that they [union leaders] can sit down on equal terms with Management."

Issue Four also described increasingly powerful efforts to recall McGrath from the USWA–CIO presidency, including the threatened resignation of the union's general counsel, Harry Sacher, because of McGrath's refusal to deal fairly with the election fraud charges. McGrath's own local had called for his recall as president of the USWA–CIO, and an article notes that the Ohio Valley District Council voted unanimously to second this resolution.

The lead story of Issue Five (July, 1946) reported on the meeting of delegates from the Shoe Worker locals of Kentucky, West Virginia and Ohio in an all-day meeting in Portsmouth. As president of the Ohio Valley Council, George Martin reported on the work of the district in the fourteen months since the previous conference. The delegates supported naming Jack Kroll, president of Ohio CIO, as National Chairman of CIO–PAC (Political Action Committee), succeeding the late Sidney Hillman. George Martin's column again moved from the local to the national, this time speaking out against a recent racist killing, apparently committed by the Ku Klux Klan.

> Our heart cried out with pain at the monstrous crime committed the other day in our land of the free, when two Negro couples were horribly murdered in Georgia by a group of white men. Because my skin is white I feel a terrible shame, don't you[?] Think! Think how twelve million American Negroes feel. Think how you would feel if some murderer was running around loose in your neighborhood threatening the lives of those near and dear to you.

He went on to quote Eleanor Roosevelt in her column "My Day" from July 29, 1946:

> "How can we talk about democracy when groups such as this mock the principle on which it is founded? ... People who can think that such actions are right are dangerous in any community and, since they cannot control themselves, they should be permanently restrained by their government."

George Martin concluded, "More than protests are necessary to remove this shame from our country. Every discriminatory practice in our own community should be wiped out."

This extraordinary piece of writing warrants a moment of appreciation: it moves from vivid first person and expressions of painful emotion ("because my skin is white I feel a terrible shame") to an appeal to the reader for empathy ("Think how you would feel") to a demonstration that a beloved national figure (Mrs. Roosevelt) endorsed these views, to a conclusion outlining what his readers must do in their own community.

Issue Six (August, 1946) brought the focus back to the national CIO scene, reporting on the election of Ohio Valley delegates to the USWA–CIO national convention scheduled for October in Atlantic City. With the November national elections fast approaching, George Martin urged his readers to see the connection between their bread-and-butter interests and national politics.

> To get wage increases, good piece work prices, protect our seniority, prevent any discharge, make our jobs secure, that we have learned. But we still have not learned that we are a part of our country and that every action [that] takes place in the halls of legislation, be it in our own community in Portsmouth, Logan, Nelsonville, or in our State Capital or State Legislature or in Congress is very much our concern.... *We must learn to understand that even the foreign policies of our country, even the kind of relations that our country has with other countries, is deeply our concern.*

These national and international matters were vital to workers' lives and families: Alluding to a peace conference about to open in Paris, George Martin turned to matters of concern to parents of twelve-year olds: "Ask this mother, this delegate sitting right here whether she wants her boy to carry a gun six years from now to go off to war and she will be sick at heart." He concluded: *"Can't you see how simple it is why we must take a deep personal interest in what's going on in this country and in the world?"*

Issue Seven (September, 1946) was the election issue, featuring statements by, and pictures of, ten civic leaders on the importance of voting. There was also an article on the State CIO Convention in Akron, Ohio, with its 900 delegates, at which George Martin was reelected vice president of the State USWA–CIO, while continuing as president of Ohio Valley District Council 2. The convention adopted an anti-Cold-War resolution that the United States, Great Britain and Russia "recapture that splendid unity of action and solidarity of the war and work out a program of perpetual peace," also demanding that no two of the Big Three powers unite "in an alliance" against the third.

Issue Eight (October, 1946) reported on the biennial National Convention of the entire USWA–CIO in Atlantic City and the plans made there for the election of a new president. The editor (George Martin) spoke with pride of the Ohio Valley delegation's teamwork:

> Since we have learned to consult with each other and not take each other for granted we copied the practice of the football team and immediately after the adjournment of each session, 33 of us from the Ohio Valley hurriedly gathered in a circle to receive announcements or act on questions of importance. Our entire membership will approve of this kind of team work and you would have enjoyed, I am sure, watching it in practice.

George Martin's column radiated confidence that the tide had turned against Frank McGrath. The election proved him right: McGrath was defeated.

Issue Nine (November, 1946) jubilantly announced McGrath's defeat. It also celebrated the reinstatement of Emerson Pence as National Representative and the reinstatement of George Martin as Regional Director, which restored him to the position in the national USWA–CIO that he had held until the intervention of the McGrath office in the summer and fall of 1945.

The tenth, eleventh, and twelfth issues (December, 1946; January, 1947; February, 1947) were full of local union affairs, including a report on gains in a new contract with Selby Shoes. George Martin's column in Issue Eleven was particularly upbeat, reporting on a meeting of the National Executive Committee of USWA–CIO: this, he said, "I believe was the first of its kind in the history of our Union and marks the true beginning of a collective leadership in our National Union." The national leaders mentioned included Vice President Julius Crane and six regional directors including George Martin himself.

Gene has some vivid memories of Dad's activities in the union. He recalls that Dad often turned union meetings into semi-cultural events, for instance playing the recording of Paul Robeson singing Earl Robinson's famous "Ballad for Americans" at one meeting. Gene also remembers that when the head of the Selby Shoe Company refurbished his office, Dad rented a garage across the street from that office and made it the union headquarters. He had a huge United Shoe Workers of America sign constructed and placed outside the headquarters, so that the boss would see it from his office window. According to another of Gene's memories, at one point during the strike Dad proposed a march to city hall. When he was told that a parade permit was needed, he announced to the large group of workers around him, "Come on everyone, we'll march to get a parade permit." Gene also recalls being concerned about spending money in a restaurant, and asking Dad about that. Dad's reply was not to worry: "It's another victory for the working classes."

THE FBI AND HUAC

Starting in 1947 the infamous HUAC—the House Un-American Activities Committee—conducted investigations (aided by the FBI) and held hearings throughout the United States, ostensibly to investigate the danger of Communist subversion. The "witch hunt" conducted by HUAC and the FBI created real terror in its first years. It showed its power in winning a perjury conviction in 1950 against

Alger Hiss, a State Department official accused of being a Soviet spy, and especially in the notorious hearings of the "Hollywood Ten": a group of ten Hollywood writers, actors, and directors who were subsequently "blacklisted" by the Hollywood studios, labeled as Communist sympathizers, and refused employment. Almost any attention from HUAC meant the blacklist. Without a chance to clear his name, a witness would suddenly find himself without friends and without a job. The extent of the damage, beyond the famous ten, can be seen in the fact that more than 300 artists—including such prominent individuals as Charlie Chaplin—were systematically denied work by the movie studios. It is estimated that only about 10% of these artists were able to rebuild their careers subsequently.

George Martin was investigated by the FBI during this period—and in fact had been under scrutiny as early as 1941. In an "information sheet" from the files of the Committee on Un-American Activities of the US House of Representatives, dated 10 March 1947, George Martin is identified as "Business Agent, Boot and Shoe Union" and "chairman of the Philadelphia Committee of the American Society for Technical Aid to Spanish Democracy, according to the letterhead of that organization." That organization had been cited as "a Communist front organization" by the Special Committee on Un-American Activities in a report dated March 29, 1944. The 1944 report continues:

> Among the signers of the Communist Party Election Petitions for Pennsylvania, 1940, was a George Martin who gave his address as M and Bristol Streets, Philadelphia. A report of 9 September 1941 by one of the investigators of the Special Committee on Un-American Activities reads:
>
> *District Organizer George Martin, Carl Mackley Apartments, M and Bristol Streets, Phila, PA. Subject is listed as a Communist in the files of the P.M.P [?] Harrisburg, PA. Confidential informant advises that subject is a Member of the Communist Party. Subject under his right name and ad-*

> *dress signed Communist Election Petition to place the Communist Party on the Ballot in Pennsylvania. This petition was signed by the subject during the early part of July, 1940.*
>
> *A George Martin of Chicago contributed an article entitled, "The Cops Were on the Job" to the <u>New Masses</u> of September 17, 1935, pp. 17–18. According to his article in this Communist periodical, Martin was arrested in August, 1931 in Chicago at a meeting called by several organizations in "opposition to the conquest of Ethiopia in particular and to war in general."*
>
> *The Communist organ, <u>The Daily Worker</u>, for April 7, 1934, p. 3 mentions a George Martin of New York who was an organizer in the Shoe Workers Repair Department of the United Shoe and Leather Workers Union.*

As far as I know, these investigations never led to George Martin being called to testify before HUAC. I do however remember an occasion on which agents of the FBI came to our home in Cincinnati— I was home at the time and was asked to go to another part of the house. I don't recall that the matter was ever discussed, but it was clearly a time of grave concern.

The fever eventually broke. By the late 1950's HUAC and the "red scare" were on the decline, to the point that HUAC was denounced by former president Harry Truman in 1959 as the "most un-American thing in the country today." But this recognition did not come until after the red scare had cost George Martin his career.

The 1949 Strike at the Selby Shoe Factory

The climax of Dad's years of union organizing was the successful strike in May 1949 against the Selby Shoe Company. Nine years later, in 1958, I wrote a term paper for a sociology course at Haverford College on the subject of that 1949 strike. To prepare for writing the paper, I collected print materials and interviewed Dad at length. I still have that paper, and I include the complete text as Appendix 2.

The essay chronicles the workings of the Selby strike from beginning to end, and it shows the careful organization and knowledge of human and group behavior needed to carry out an action of this sort.

The issue at the heart of the strike was the union call to amend their contract to establish a guaranteed average minimum wage—a long-term strategy designed to ensure that worker pay would be protected from changes in the piecework rate.

The essay argues that the key to the union's success was its ability to recognize certain aspects of group behavior and use them to its advantage. Some of the groundwork was laid long before the strike, including the *Champion*'s earlier coverage of the successful Nelsonville/Brooks strike, which communicated the benefits and the excitement of a successful action. Careful planning in the immediate run-up to the Selby strike ensured broad participation and support among union members: strategies included soliciting input about demands and tactics from the rank and file, establishing clearly defined objectives, and using the company's own strike preparations to help foster loyalty and group solidarity.

When the walkout began, union leaders used careful staging to set the tone for the strike and bolster the workers' enthusiasm and sense of purpose. And during the long haul of the strike itself, the union maintained worker morale and countered company offensives in a variety of ways. These ranged from providing support for workers who were in financial difficulty to anticipating and planning for moments when workers would be most vulnerable to company messages.

Late in the strike, the company tried to discredit George Martin by mining his biography for what they hoped would be damaging details. The company prepared an exposé that described the Regional Director as an unelected outsider come to sow dissension between the company and its workers. Even more, they said, he was a Jewish immigrant with subversive connections, who was apparently operating under an alias, since he had changed his name after arriving in the United States. The would-be exposé had little impact, however. George Martin got wind of it in advance and published the most potentially damaging accusations himself, along with explanations, and sent a copy to every striking worker. The smear campaign ended up backfiring on the company.

After nine weeks of attack and counter-attack, the union and Selby Shoes reached a settlement. The workers got their guaranteed wage, a new contract was approved, and work resumed at the factory.

There is an archive on the 1949 Selby strike in the Robert E. and Jean R. Mahn Center for Archives and Special Collections at the Ohio University library.

[5]
1949–1972: CINCINNATI

WE MOVED TO AN apartment on Reading Road in Cincinnati in the summer of 1949. I'm not sure why we moved at that time, but it was probably in part because of the school situation. Lower Dry Run School, which Gene and I attended, had no eighth grade. Gene remembers that the Howard girls, who lived next door to us, didn't go to school beyond the seventh grade. Gene was to start eighth grade in the Fall of 1949, and in Cincinnati he could attend Walnut Hills High School, a college preparatory public school modeled on the Boston Latin School. Mom and Dad knew a couple in Cincinnati named Fanny and Albert Barnett (teachers of mathematics, she at Walnut Hills, he at the University of Cincinnati) who were building a new home. We arranged to purchase their old home on Sturgis Avenue in North Avondale. We lived in the apartment on Reading Road while waiting for their house to be available. In fall 1949, I entered the fourth grade at the North Avondale School, near Sturgis Avenue.

Meanwhile, Dad and Mom put the Coles Park house on the market. It had been purchased in 1946 for $6,250. They were still trying to sell it in early 1951 for $6,500.

Figure 9: George and Sylvia on a vacation trip (date and location unknown)

The move was also convenient for Dad's work in the North. He had become president of the five-state council (and was still CIO National Representative) and therefore travelled frequently to USWA locals in Wisconsin, Michigan, and Minnesota. Also, Mom had better teaching opportunities in Cincinnati. She worked at Central High School in Cincinnati (a vocational school), Withrow High School, and later at Walnut Hills. She returned to graduate school, completing an MA in history at the University of Cincinnati in 1950 with a thesis on the *London Times*' coverage of the Spanish Civil War of 1936.

We had other good friends in Cincinnati, including Jay and Charlotte Paradise and Herman and Susan Freudenthal. Jay Paradise was a labor lawyer who represented the Brewery Workers of America. The Freudenthals had come to the United States from Germany before World War II; we became friends when a postman mistakenly delivered to them a left-wing paper (I think it was the I.F. Stone *Weekly*) meant for us (or vice versa).

The move to Cincinnati must have marked a welcome change for Mom and Dad—it was the start of a life with the friendship of more kindred spirits, and more concerts and more cultural activities of all sorts. They had subscription tickets for the Cincinnati Symphony Orchestra, which they attended every Saturday evening. The Sturgis Avenue house, once we moved into it, seemed quite wonderful to all of us. Dad started a garden in the back yard and built a brick patio. In the summers we traveled to the "borscht belt" of New York to a small summer resort called Pine Lake Lodge owned and operated by Dad's sisters Manya (and her husband, Abram Hamburger) and Dora (and her husband Sam Kokot). Gene and I stayed at Pine Lake Lodge, Gene as a busboy in the kitchen, for several summers. The time there brought us in touch with Dad's sisters Manya and Dora, who had brought him to the United States, and their families, including two sons-in-law who had fought against the Franco regime in the Spanish Civil War as part of the Abraham Lincoln Brigade in 1936.[4] We became acquainted in those summers with the Yiddish-speaking left-wing community of New York City, the Hamburgers' friends and clientele at Pine Lake Lodge.

Dad's work continued through 1951, taking him often to Shoeworker locals in Saint Paul, Minnesota, Stillwater, Michigan, and Red Wing, Wisconsin. The storm of anti-Communist "purge" activities within the union leadership continued to rage,[5] and having been labeled and suspected for so many years, Dad fought a losing battle to continue his life's work. By early February Dad's job had come to an end. It clearly came as no surprise to him, and he took it in stride. The letter he wrote to his sister, Manya, on Feb. 9, 1952, has no self-pity:

> About myself: It looks as if my job is no more. The question now is whether I will continue to get pay till March 15 or till May 1st. I

[4.] Manya and Abram Hamburger had two children: Anna and Naomi. Anna (and Al Warren) had three children: Fred, Connie and David. Naomi (and Maury Colow) had two children: Alix and Josh. Dora and Sam Kokat had one child: Judy. Judy (and Stanley Weisburger) had two children: Devra and Ellen. Appendix 3 is a partial family genealogy.

[5.] See Appendix 4, a retrospective on the "Communist-dominated" unions.

got wind of some of the underhanded deals and my dismissal will "prove that some bastard is a full fledged skunk and legitimate bastard and not to be trusted from here on..." You need not guess Manya Dear how low Rosenburg will sink. A few weeks ago, the Nat'l Ex Com. met in Wash. And a delegation from N.Y. leadership came and asked for unanimous O.K. to endorse R. for Nat'l Pres. of the Union since he is most qualified to get rid of the few communists left and keep them out. R. took the floor to assure all that he can do it just as good as Quill etc. And when he got thru, Senator McCarthy and Pegler looked like "lemoshkes" compared to him. I am without any assignment so I am busy getting my records in shape and soon will begin looking for a job. All suggestions from every member of the family will be carefully considered and the winning suggestion on how I can best storm the business industry and commercial world will receive a grand prize. It is a lot of fun to be home with the family and help my "big three" rush out for school every morning and be on hand for their return and listen to their daily experiences.

It took Dad several months to find another job. A Cincinnati friend of the family named Mike Israel, a prominent and wealthy neighbor, helped Dad get a job with a clothing firm called Ironall Pants that I believe he owned. A better job came along through our friend Jay Paradise, who helped him become the administrator of the newly negotiated pension fund set up by the Brewery Workers Union and Standard Brands as part of a strike settlement. Working alone in a small office in a large office building in downtown Cincinnati, Dad administered the claims and pension payments under the plan. I think there was little of interest in the job, but Dad took pleasure in helping workers navigate the bureaucratic red tape, making sure they got all they were entitled to. He went to the local YMCA gym during his lunch break; I joined him on several occasions in the late 50s and 60s when I was home from college.

Much of Dad's life in these years revolved around family trips, often to Arizona to visit Mom's parents in Tucson, Arizona, and to the East Coast to visit Dad's relatives in Bensonhurst, Brooklyn, and Mom's sister in Springfield, Massachusetts, and then in Rutherford, New Jersey. Dad played a role in organizing the Golden Wedding Anniversary of his sister Manya and her husband Abram in Bensonhurst in February, 1959.

Dad became increasingly involved in local Democratic politics in Cincinnati. In 1964 he was elected Precinct Executive of Democratic Party, Ward 13, Precinct DD. There is a Block Report for August 1964 with every street and every house listed. He helped elect John Gilligan to Congress in November 1964. Gilligan wrote: "Dear George: ... if every Precinct Executive in Hamilton County worked his precinct the way you do, there wouldn't be a Republican elected to office for the next fifty years."

This was also a time of reconnecting with relatives from abroad. For example, in September of 1964, Dad's nephew Elimelech Schory

Figure 10: In Cincinnati with the local Neighborhood Council of the Democratic Party

(son of his sister Hayablima) visited from Israel. Dad arranged for Manya to join the celebration, and for me to come from the East Coast to join them. Dad and Mom returned the visit to Israel in June, 1965.

Dad's 1963 passport indicates a good deal of travel, all family-related: Belgium and France in 1963, France and Israel in 1965, and Brazil, Peru, Chile and Argentina in 1967. His 1970 passport shows travel to Ghana, Togo, and Cote D'Ivoire in 1970, to visit Gene and family.

The last time I saw Dad was late in the summer of 1972 in Cincinnati. Katherine and I were preparing to go to Taiwan for a full year,

Figure 11: On the kibbutz in 1965. Manya in center

where Katherine would do research for her Ph.D. dissertation and I would teach philosophy at the National Taiwan University. Dad was already quite ill. I believe it was clear that he had pancreatic cancer, but he didn't acknowledge it, at least to me. (Gene tells me that he learned fairly recently from his son Seth that Dad told then ten-year-old Seth that he was dying, while the two of them were taking a walk.) Standing at the foot of his bed, I told Dad that we could delay or cancel the trip because of his illness. He cut me off abruptly, saying that was out of the question—that he would be fine. Because it wasn't clear to me that he knew the seriousness of his condition, his comment was difficult to respond to. Without a doubt, he wanted us to continue with the adventures of our lives.

Dad died on November 3, 1972, at the Jewish Hospital in Cincinnati, Ohio. His death certificate listed his occupation as "Labor Organizer-Trade Union." A memorial was held on November 19, 1972. The cover of the memorial program has a picture of Dad holding Eric—who looks to be about 3 years old—in his arms. The memorial program was as follows:

Robert Martin: Sarabande, Suite in C Major—J.S. Bach

Theodore M. Berry, Mayor Elect of Cincinnati

William K. Billingsley

Martin Bloom [Dad's brother-in-law]

William F. Bowen, State Senator

William J. Chenault, Vice-Mayor of Cincinnati

Maury Colow [husband of Dad's niece[

William Garnes, Director, Ohio Bureau of Unemployment Compensation

George C. Hale, M.D.

John E. Hansan, Assistant to the Governor of Ohio,
representing Governor John J. Gilligan

C.E. (Mike) Israel

Thomas A. Luken, Mayor of Cincinnati

Eugene V. Martin

Fred Swenty

Charles Thomson, President, Sturgis Avenue Block Club

Sidney Weil, Co-Chairman, Hamilton County Democratic Party

John Wiethe, Co-Chairman, Hamilton County Democratic Party

James C. Paradise, presiding

Ralph Marcus [Dad's friend, an organizer from the UE (Electrical Workers), and
later husband of Sylvia, who gave an impassioned speech]

Sarabande, Suite in D minor—J.S. Bach

[6]

Concluding Comment

DEAR Seth, Eric, Jeremy, Louisa, Benjamin, Emily, Jane, George, Rachel, Sarah, Vincent, Edda, Felix, and Ruben:

As I end this account of your grandfather and great-grandfather, my thoughts return to the feelings I had at Dad's bedside the last time I saw him. He was in control of the situation. He left no doubt that we were to stick with our plans, to take advantage of the opportunities we had, to make the most of our lives. This applies to you. He loved the grandchildren born while he was alive—Seth, Eric, Jeremy, Louisa—and he would have loved the rest of you and your children. Your lives are a continuation of his. He would be enormously proud of you. He would save programs of your school activities, your graduations, your every accomplishment. I hope his love and pride give you strength and confidence as you make the most of your lives.

Figure 12: In the backyard in Cincinnati, ca. 1970

Appendix I: A Visit To Sosnowiec (2008)

During a trip to various cities in eastern Europe for the Bard Conservatory in January, Katherine and I spent a day visiting the small city of Sosnowiec (this is the Polish spelling; in Yiddish I think it is Sosnowitz), where Dad was born and where he lived until he was nineteen. Here is an account of the day.

WE MET ARTUR SZYNDLER at 9 a.m. on Sunday, January 20, 2008 at our hotel in Krakow. He had been recommended to us as a guide to Sosnowiec and as someone who could do research for us, by Kate Craddy, director of the Galicia Jewish Museum in Krakow. Artur is a young man—late thirties (?), married, with a nine year old daughter, pleasant, a bit shy, rather large, dressed like a student with a day pack over his shoulder. The material we had tried to send him—power of attorney, copies of pages from Dad's 1937 Polish passport—hadn't made it through the fax, but he had obtained two pre-war maps of Sosnowiec, as I requested, one from 1907, the other from 1936. After looking at the maps for a while, he and Katherine and I set out in his car.

We drove west for more than an hour through sparsely wooded, flat terrain. The day was grey and drizzling. As we neared Katowice we turned north for the short drive to Sosnowiec, a small city—it seemed somewhat smaller than Kingston, N.Y., near us. As we drove toward the center we saw many Communist-era cement apartment buildings—10 or 12 stories high—close together. We were in the center very quickly—it was marked by an attractive classical style train station (with a date of 1869, I think). Artur had told us that the area across from the station—principally one long street (Modrzejowska) and several side streets (Kolejowa and Targowa)—was the pre-war Jewish section of Sosnowiec. In the pre-war period, Sosnowiec had a population of about 130,000 of which more than 20% were Jews. We parked and walked into that section. As opposed to Krakow, nothing in the Jewish quarter is now marked as such. The only historical marker I saw was a statue of an opera singer from Sosnowiec, famous in the 1920s and 30s, marking a small plaza opposite the train station.

We walked down the main street (Modrzejowska), filled with shops on the lower levels of mostly attractive buildings that appeared to date from the 19th century. About two blocks on the right we saw a building that Artur identified as the synagogue (though there is no indication now that it is or was once a synagogue). We turned into one of the previously identified side streets. Some buildings were in good repair, others dark and in poor repair. (I took pictures of both kinds of buildings, always wondering if one was the building in which the Gotfried family lived.) We stepped into the courtyards of several of these and saw the typical scenes—small balconies of 4 or 5-story apartment buildings. In one courtyard we saw the row of small rooms used to store coal for the winters. The streets were relatively quiet with a handful of people, alone or in small groups, heading one way or another.

We went back to the car and drove to the Jewish cemetery of Sosnowiec. This cemetery was established in the late 19th century and shows up plainly—adjacent to the Catholic cemetery—in our prewar map. It was difficult for Artur to find—there are no signs or markers. Finally, after asking people on the street, he stopped at a small flower stand at the end of a small road and asked the proprietor, then parked. The flower stand owner produced a key and let us into the Jewish cemetery. As we entered, family groups were also entering the Catholic cemetery. We were the only visitors to the Jewish cemetery while we were there. The Jewish cemetery is somewhat smaller than a football field. Though untended and dilapidated, it did not show signs of vandalism. Some of the graves had flowers placed on them. One large plaque near the entrance has a message in Polish and Hebrew commemorating "members of the community who were murdered by Hitler between 1939 and 1944." There were graves from various periods—including one from 2003 (!)—and many from the 20s and 30s. In all, surprisingly few gravestones, and toward the back, much open land.

From the cemetery we drove to the site of the ghetto of Bedzin and Sosnowiec, located in the area called "Schrodel" (Srodula). Artur provided us with a copy of small Nazi map of the ghetto, dated April, 1943. As I understand it from book entries on Sosnowiec, the Germans entered Sosnowiec in September, 1939 and immediately attacked the Jews, setting fire to the Great Synagogue. More than 10,000 Jews were deported to nearby Auschwitz-Birkenau (near Krakow). The Nazis built two ghettos, one in Srodula (where we were) and the other in "old Sosnowiec." (?) Starting in May, 1943, the Jews were taken from these ghettos to Auschwitz-Birkenau. The ghetto structures in Srodula were completely destroyed—the area is now a park-playground with a single small stone memorial marker.

The visit to the ghetto memorial ended our visit—we drove back to Krakow, mostly in silence. We had lunch together at our hotel in Krakow. We learned that Artur (clearly not Jewish, though we didn't ask) grew up in Oswiecim (Polish for Auschwitz). His father was an engineer. Artur studied history of religion ("the science of religion" as I believe it is called, indicating a scientific, i.e., secular, perspective) at the Jagellonian University in Krakow. His interest in local history led him to a specialization in the history of the Jews of the region (he commented that there hadn't been much done on that particular topic), including pre-Holocaust history. He finished his doctorate and is now head of research at the Auschwitz Jewish Center (at the site of the death camp), currently working on a project involving Sosnowiec, among other things. His main work is to give talks to visitors to Auschwitz—of which there are very large numbers. Artur told us that the three almost adjacent locations—Krakow, Sosnowiec, and Katowice—were in pre-war days part of three different countries: Krakow (and the rest of Galicia) was part of the Austro-Hungarian Empire; Sosnowiec (and the broader region called Zaglabia) was officially part of Russia; Katowice (and the rest of Silesia) was part of Prussia. After World War I, in 1918, all three areas became part of (reestablished) Poland. Sosnowiec and Krakow are are now part of the province of Silesia, whose records are kept in Katowice. (We learned, incidentally, that there was military conscription throughout this period—perhaps relevant to Dad's having left Poland at the age of 19?) Artur told us what materials might be available to assist in genealogical research:

1. Vital records—birth, marriage, death
2. Census documents (collected periodically)
3. Tax records
4. Voting lists (for the Polish Parliament and the City Councils)
5. Business directories from the 20s and 30s (like our Yellow Pages)
6. Lists (kept by the Nazis) of Jews in the Sosnowiec ghettos
7. A file on the Bund, which worked with Polish socialist groups

This last item was mentioned by Artur in response to my questions about the Bund's activities in Sosnowiec. There were Bund activities in Lodz, apparently—which is 194 kilometers from Sosnowiec. (I asked about this because Dad mentioned Lodz often—in fact, I had the impression for a long time that Sosnowiec was a suburb of Lodz.) As we concluded our conversation, I asked Artur to pursue three things as best he could:

1. To find a Sosnowiec street address for the Gotfried family from Dad's birth record (1904, according to his passport—but why did we have the idea that he was born in 1905?);
2. Any other information on the family (including Hamburger and Kokat), including the fate of family members in the Holocaust;
3. Information on the Bund in Sosnowiec in the period from about 1918 to 1923 (when Dad left for the United States).

We told Artur that Ben will be coming to Krakow (to the Jagellonian University) in July.

Robert Martin
—February 3, 2008

Appendix 2: "Strike, 1949"— College Paper on the 1949 Selby Strike, by Robert Martin (1958)

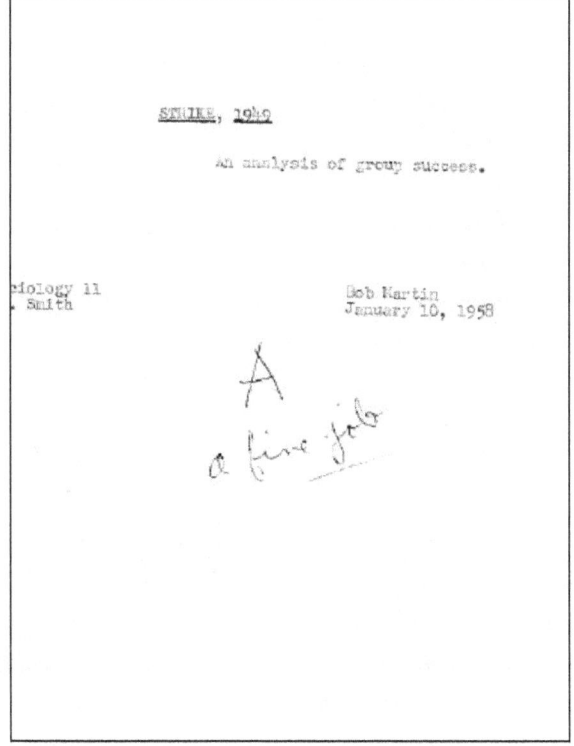

The text that follows is a scanned version of the original paper.

STRIKE, 1949
An Analysis of Group Success
Introductory Note

In May 1949, Portsmouth Ohio witnessed a strike between the Selby Shoe Company and Local #117 of the United Shoe Workers, CIO. The strike ended nine weeks later with the concession by the Company to the major union demands. The following is a study of the way in which this strike was won.

Objectivity, that prized and almost impossible attitude, has no meaning here, primarily because I am not involved in a discussion of the justification or morality of either side in the conflict. I have dealt only briefly with the issues in the strike, and concentrated on the organization and tactics of the winning side.

The social relevance of a study thus limited was fortunate for me, because of the necessity of these limitations. I lived through the situation in question, and my father was its principal character--I am obviously biased in my value judgments of the situation, and if this is not clear in the paper it is because again, I am not dealing with value judgments.

Sources include a rather fragmentary personal recollection of the strike, a long, specially prepared-for interview with my father, and access to a very comprehensive documentation of the strike (newspaper clippings, complete radio speeches of both sides, a bulk of material sent by both the Company and the Union to the workers' homes, and transcripts of negotiation material).

Before investigating these sources, I read E. T. Hiller's <u>The Strike, A Study in Collective Action</u>, (University of Chicago Press, 1928) and several articles in <u>Industrial Conflict, A Psychological Interpretation</u>, (The Gordon Publishing Company, 1939) edited by G. W. Hartman and T. Newcomb for the Society for the Psychological Study of Social Issues.

In the interview with my father I secured a rather complete narration of the incidents and campaigns of this strike, purposely avoiding comments on strikes in general. From this mass of details on the Portsmouth strike and its background, I have used only what seemed to have significance in determining the outcome of the strike.

Bob Martin
January 10, 1958

STRIKE, 1949

> "...now the boss won't listen
>   when one guy squawks,
> but he's gotta' listen when
>   the Union talks--
> he'd better....
> be mighty lonely..."

(from the Talking Union, by Pete Seeger--one of the songs sung in the mass meetings of the Shoeworkers' strike)

Portsmouth, located at the meeting of the Scioto and Ohio Rivers in South-Central Ohio, had a population of about forty thousand in 1949. Three plants dominated the city's industry--a steel mill and two shoe factories. Williams Shoe, with about thirteen hundred employees, was the newer of the two, and non-union. Selby's, one of Portsmouth's first concerns (founded 1877 by G. D. Selby), employed about twenty-four hundred men and women, turned out an average of nine thousand pairs of shoes a day, and was organized in 1942 by the United Shoe Workers, a part of the CIO. Many earlier attempts had been made to organize the plant--the AFL Boot and Shoe Workers made many early, unsuccessful, bids and in 1937, soon after the formation of the CIO, a representative of that Union formed a Local in Portsmouth.

A strike was crushed--the Local maintained a token membership of about 75, and was recognized as representative for only this tiny minority. A renewed drive began in 1941 (under most of the same leaders who would lead the 1949 strike), and a strike won in 1942 established the Union as sole representative and brought a pay increase. In the following years, good labor-management relations prevailed. For example, the November 1946 issue of the Shoe Workers' Champion carried this item, headlined "HATS OFF":

> To Mr. N. B. Griffin, President of the Selby Shoe Company, who made this statement before the Kiwanis Club: "We are operating under a Union shop and for the first six months of the agreement it has been successful. People are working with good feeling and we have had no difficulty with slowing down of production."

In March of 1947, the "good feelings" were expressed in a full two page Selby ad in the Champion. Under a bold-faced heading, "GOOD UNION RELATIONS," it said, in part:

> We believe that sensible operation and administration . . . by Union officers and management has helped make it possible for workers and management, working together, to reach some goals that seemed desirable a year ago. As our relationship matures, we can expect even greater accomplishments.

The Portsmouth public, one tenth of whom had direct financial interest in Selbys, were happy with the Union--town merchants prospered in the good labor-management relationship. A birthday issue of

the <u>Champion</u> carried birthday greetings from the
local department store, jewelry store, five and ten,
restaurants, hotels, markets, a funeral home, and a
bank. Son's Grill, boasting of the "Smartest Cocktail Lounge in Portsmouth," stated their position in
capital letters:

                    FOR LABOR
                    BY LABOR
                    OF LABOR

    The formal structures of Selbys and Local 117 were fairly typical. Roger Selby held controlling stock in the Company and was President of the Board of Directors. A staff of experts managed the Company--a President, labor relations man, efficiency expert, and other technical engineers. There was a completely defined formal hierarchy of (descending) General Supervisors, Department Supervisors, Shop Supervisors, Shop Foremen, and Assistant Foremen. This structure was rather rigidly maintained in dealings with the Union as well as in the routine operations of the plant.

    The Union had a slightly more complex formal structure. The Local (117) had a President, Secretary-Treasurer, and three Trustees as officers, and an Executive Board of about 25 members. All were elected from the Local, and only the President and Secretary-Treasurer gave up factory jobs to work full time on the Local payroll. The rest of the Local was structured around the plant--a Steward was elected in each shop (fitters, cutters, etc.). The entire Local met once a month, the Executive Board every week, and the officers carried on the day to day work. 117 was of course part of a larger structure, the United Shoe Workers, which in turn was a branch of the CIO. The Washington office of the Shoe Workers employed a director to supervise and advise Locals in Ohio, West Virginia, and Kentucky.

The tension developing in Portsmouth caused some slight informal readjustments in structure. The Local leadership, while supported by the members and capable of managing the day to day affairs, was composed of shoe workers, and not trade-union tacticians. They were joined in the early contract negotiation difficulties by the President of the national Union, and the Regional Director already mentioned. The Regional Director played a very important leading role in the strike that followed, despite his official advisory position.

A few more points are of importance for this background of the strike to be considered. In the six years from 1943 (the successful strike that established the Union) to 1949, the Union had built up very good relations with the general membership, and prepared the people for what was perhaps to come. The Local had baseball, basketball, and bowling teams (also leagues for the kids on Saturday mornings) and a monthly paper, the Champion. (It was discontinued during the strike.) Members of the Local were active in National Labor Movement functions, attending conventions, and winning positions. A strong sense of "unionism" had been developed--for example, a strike, followed dramatically in the Champion, between the Shoeworkers in Nelsonville Ohio and the Brooks Shoe Company (1947) aroused Union feelings and discussed ideas that were to be of great importance in Portsmouth later. Open letters from strikers were published, and emotionalized headlines won the interest and sympathy of the Portsmouth workers: "BROOKS SHOE PLANT STRUCK. WAGE RAISE LONG OVERDUE. STRIKERS SOLID IN FACE OF BROOKS' VIRTUAL LOCKOUT." Front page editorials strengthened Union values:

> Brooks Shoe Workers . . . are going to prove to their employers that this is Nelsonville, USA, in the Year of our Lord, 1947--that collective bargaining is an old American custom, that prices for the necessities of life have skyrocketed while earnings are unchanged-- that they intend to enjoy at least some share of the company's profits which they made possible while working for the lowest wages.

The glory of victory was emphasized and the requirements for victory made clear. "'REDS UNDER BEDS,' RELIGIOUS BAITING AND 'MOVING' SCARES FAIL TO BREAK MILITANT UNITY OF NELSONVILLE LOCAL." A front page picture caption reads: "With heads high, chests out, the victorious strikers proudly parade back to work under the banner of the Union." The success of this strike was of further importance, finally, in strengthening the worker's faith in the Regional

Director, who was important also in the Nelsonville leadership.

At a monthly meeting in 1949, the workers in Local 117 decided to improve their contract. One of the important demands, which was to become the central issue in the strike, was, briefly stated, a rewording of a piece rate clause in the contract, to insure a minimum average hourly wage no matter what piece rates were set.

This early, pre-negotiation period presented an interesting combination of rigorous democracy and skillful control. The democracy was of course important in maintaining unity, and the workers had been led to understand the necessity of granting a certain amount of freedom to their leaders. Suggestions for contract changes were collected by all Stewards from their shops and turned over for screening to the Executive Board. Another mass meeting gave negotiating power to the officers and the Regional Director, who would use the ideas drafted by the Executive Board. For reasons of strategy, this negotiating committee took complete power to formulate the actual demands for presentation at the negotiation hearings. Thus by keeping secret all the important demands of the workers, the negotiating committee could make up bluff demands, later to be dropped with an air of compromise, and still maintain the vital issues.

After each negotiation session; the leaders reported to the Local on what demands had been made, and how they had been received. Both sides used the trick of bluff issues--the Company brought forth a pay decrease, and the Union asked for a large increase, but after a great show of good will the Company insisted on a complete contract renewal, and the Union demanded a rewording of the piece-rate clause. The workers had frequent votes to show approval of the negotiating committee, and frequent speeches dramatized the problems, in rather clever, non-technical terms. In one such mass meeting speech, the Regional Director compared a minority of the workers' desire to concentrate on a simple pay raise instead of the rewording of the piece rate clause, to the idea of putting new furniture in a house with a leak. The furniture would be ruined by the seeping water, just as wage increases would be lost in altered piece rates if there were no average hourly guarantee, and surely the Union should patch this hole before winning more pay. All these preliminary discussions, meetings, votes, explanations, etc., were of great importance in solidifying the group and clearly defining its objectives; the mere unity of the group was not enough--with just "togetherness" they could stage a "back to work" against the Union, or turn against the leadership, or give in early in the strike. From the very beginning of the tension the importance of their demands was underlined constantly, to set very clear goals for the group action.

A short time before the contract expiration (which, incidentally, outlawed strikes during its term), the mounting tension began to focus around the now-expected strike. Quiet Company preparations actually strengthened the Union. First, foremen began to ask for overtime work, supposedly to meet some special "rush" orders. Given the required one-day notice, the workers were forced by the present contract to accept, but they chose to believe that the Company was building its arsenal for the strike--stocking up heavily in preparation. The bad effect of this--many workers refusing the overtime in violation of the contract--was carefully cut to a minimum; the men were personally urged by the Union leaders to remain loyal to their fellow-workers and abide by the contract for the few remaining days--"then we'll show 'em." The Company's action had another very positive effect--it made the workers feel that the strike was being forced upon them. This kind of defensive, back-against-the-wall feeling is probably very conducive to a good fight.

A day later the shop foremen asked all workers for addresses and telephone numbers. The workers took this as an obvious sign that the Company would not give in in the negotiations and were getting ready for a strike; of course the addresses were used for mailing Company "literature" to the striking workers later. The effect here was much the same as that just mentioned. (Further Company preparations were felt only later in the strike--they were ready on the first day with carefully prepared radio speeches, pamphlets, press releases etc., and initiated amazingly organized offensives at each stage of the strike.)

The Union was in no great hurry to begin the strike--they violated one fairly general rule in strike tactics to follow another more important one. Usually strikes are called as early as possible to give the Company a minimum of time to prepare. In this case, however, the Union found it very comfortable to wait--it was the month of May, and in the weeks ahead the shoe business would pick up to its highest pace, preparing for the big fall season. A summer strike could be most crippling--no Company wants to be struck when profits could be at a maximum, and, again in the worker's favor, there would be no abundance of unemployed shoe workers who could be tempted to work in the struck plant.

So while waiting calmly, a mass meeting unanimously resolved that if the new contract were not signed, a walkout would begin at the expiration of the present one. As the workers left the hall, the Executive Board members, Stewards, and officers were asked to remain. The strike organization was set up quickly and simply with the emphasis on personal importance, responsibility, and urgency. Each Steward was a picket-captain and assigned to a factory gate--he devised a rotating picket schedule. The strength of the relatively primary relationships that grow from working in the same specialized shop was recognized and used in the shop-organization of picketing. Fund raising, relief distribution, radio, and newspaper release committees were formed, besides the very important special walkout committee.

Negotiations ended in a deadlock--the strike was set for the following day at noon. The walkout is described in detail, for it appears to be of great importance in understanding the success of the strike; the walkout set a tone that was most carefully maintained for the entire nine weeks of the strike. The walkout committee, 5 popular workers, was divided so that two led the way out at the appointed time, going from shop to shop, and three stayed behind to be last out--to make sure none stayed behind.

The natural group feelings of the workers, a readiness and happiness to be identified with & strong collective movement, were carefully reinforced. The walkout committee was instructed to make quite a scene; their briefing included orders to "smile, yell, be happy, call the workers by name, make a lot of noise, get a holiday spirit going-- tell the people they're going on vacation."

The walkout was a great success--the workers paraded as instructed across the street to the union hall, yelling and slapping each other on the back. The waiting officers called off the names of each shop in order, and each Steward in turn stepped forward and yelled, "One hundred percent," amid wild cheers.

At the height of the excitement the Regional Director mounted the platform and gave a short speech. He congratulated the workers on their courage and unity, and, playing on their feelings of solidarity and responsibility, predicted that the whole community would be watching them, and that they must act without destructiveness or maliciousness. Always emphasizing their position in the group, their collectivity and their reflections upon one another, he urged them to confine whatever drinking they did to their homes (the implication of "holiday spirit" had to be controlled) and to respect the property rights of the community. He warned them of a tremendous flood of Company propaganda that would fall upon them, and warned them not to listen to rumors and gossip. Ending dramatically, he called for volunteers for picketing (even though complete picketing schedules had already been made out) and the entire Local stepped forward with a burst of cheering. With final instructions (mass meetings were once a week now) the meeting was adjourned and the workers went home.

The strike problems faced by the Union can be divided into two groups--maintaining morale and meeting Company offensives. Of course the two were very closely related (an unmet Company offensive would certainly weaken morale, for example) but the most significant incidents and policies can be classified in this way.

Of course the greatest factor in keeping up morale was the background of successful unionism--there was to start with a very unified, self-aware group. This psychological strength was very important, especially since the treasury was low. A relief committee heard in complete privacy the cases of workers who couldn't pay rent or buy food. Merchants and farmers contributed products, and a kitchen was set up in the Union office to serve hot coffee and sandwiches to the pickets. Letters of encouragement were mailed at short intervals--at mass meetings, outside speakers were brought in to add prestige to the strike, spirits were raised by carefully developed talks, Union songs were sung, and skits put on. Radio time and newspaper space was bought to give the workers encouraging reports on the settlement progress. The workers were assembled as much as possible into all kinds of groups and committees. Discouragement and personal suffering is felt much more strongly alone, and in groups the workers strengthened each other. Monday morning is always a dangerous time for morale. Monday was the day to go back to work--a lifetime of factory work had conditioned into all a half-instinctive impulse to return, and the Company played on this. To counteract this, there was special "Monday morning mobilization" every week of the strike--greater picket squads--30 or 40 instead of five and six--guarded the gates.

The greatest part of the Union battle can be

discussed under the second classification of problems, that of catching the Company's moves. For example, in the first week of the strike the workers had to return to the plant to receive their paychecks for the week before. The President, without any propaganda, sent a schedule to each worker for picking up his check; they were to go in very small groups at different times of the day. During these hours the group feeling would be at its lowest, and the Union leadership would be completely out of touch with the workers. A clever Company speech could make this a very dangerous day indeed. The day before payday, each worker received from the Union some mimeographed sheets. The first page read, in part:

> TO ALL MEMBERS: To protect your job and bring the strike to a successful conclusion, be sure you take the following action: When you get your paycheck this coming Friday please contact your Steward at the Union Hall (across the street) for a very important message.

(This device was often used--the promise of a very important message usually assured good attendance, and the leadership would have a chance to counteract any Company propaganda.)

Point #2 announced a mass meeting the following Monday, #3 asked them to read carefully the enclosed statement, and #4 ended dramatically:

> Do not listen to rumors and gossip. Reject all bosses' propaganda and condemn peddlers of hate

and confusion. Attend Union meetings daily at 10 A.M. and special Mass Meeting Monday at 10.

YOURS FOR AN EARLY AND SUCCESSFUL VICTORY
Signed, President   Signed, Sec'y Treasurer

The Company opened up a brilliant campaign based on a single slogan--"Why is there a Strike at Selbys?" This was repeated at the beginning and end of every radio speech, letter, advertisement, and pamphlet. It was repeated in station breaks every hour on the radio--Why is there a strike at Selbys? A speech of May 18 opened the campaign, with the following paragraph:

> In our opinion the issues on what the strike is about are too small to justify the great losses you are suffering. We hope that you are asking yourself the big question, WHY? We regret that the strike occurred. We have done everything possible to settle the issues. We are certain it would not have happened had you had all the available facts and the opportunity of a secret ballot. Have you considered just WHY DID THE UNION LEADERS CALL THIS STRIKE?

The slogan was shortened simply to "Why," and it became the catchword of the town. The wives and children of the workers began to ask "Why?" and the workers began to ask the leadership "WHY." Then the Union took an old political campaign slogan, "HAD ENOUGH" and began thundering it to the public. Speech after speech ridiculed the Company question:

```
            The Company knows WHY
            The businessmen know WHY
            The workers know WHY
            Everyone knows WHY.
            WE'VE HAD ENOUGH
```

Again a hundred repetitions a day, in the papers and on the radio. "The Company has hired some smart people to think up gimmick slogans--why don't they say yes to the worker's needs instead of making up stupid questions? WE'VE HAD ENOUGH." Whether the Union slogan was catchier, or repeated more often, or met by a more sympathetic public, the new password in Portsmouth became "Had Enough," and the Company discontinued its station-break Why's.

A final example of the Company's strategy, and the Union counterattack, occurred near the end of the strike. To divide the strike leadership the Company chose the Regional Director for discrediting, both for his important role in the strike, and because of some factors that they felt they could use. First of all, as mentioned earlier, the Regional Director was in the formal structure, an advisor, and was one of the few officers not elected by the Local. His past work with the Union, and Local 117 in particular, had put him in a place of high respect and importance among the workers, but the Company reminded the public continually that he was not elected. He was the "outsider," and the Company claimed that he had come into Portsmouth to "wreck the town." The Regional Director was Jewish, in a town predominantly Protestant, and perhaps the only man in the town born in Europe. The Company found on citizenship papers that he had changed to his present name when he arrived in America at the age of nineteen, and in speeches they gave his name the mysterious sounding prefix, "alias." Using a charge common against the CIO at the time, he was labeled subversive, and the rest of the leadership was referred to as "his gang." Tipped off about the coming "exposé", the Regional Director secured a copy and printed it himself, with proper comments and explanations. Sending a copy to each worker completely ruined the Company's planned effect--what good is an exposed "exposé"? Causing the scandal to backfire, the <u>Champion</u> published a special issue, headlined across the page:

> UNION BUSTING EXPOSED: Spotlight turned on peddlers of hate, poison, and confusion who resort to smear tactics.

One of the most effective devices of the Union was the use of "special meetings." Three times during the nine-week strike, at moments of great importance, personal letters were sent by a member of the Union leadership to about 125 workers. These people were actually chosen at random, as long as they had at one time shown some interest in the Union. The letter emphasized the person's former loyalty, the grave position of the Union, and the need for his assistance. Would they please take time out Saturday morning to attend a special informal meeting--and not to bring anyone else. Of course, feelings of importance and exclusiveness were already aroused, and a very large percentage appeared at the meeting. At the meeting their loyalty to the group would again be raised, and new responsibility emphasized. Some fairly routine task would be assigned then (like calling five merchants each and explaining the worker's position in the strike, or taking extra picket duty) and they would be dismissed with a strong feeling of appreciation and gratitude by the leadership. Not only did the work get done, and with more vigor than usual, but each of the "selected" men felt a new, deep personal responsibility for the strike--a new enthusiasm permeated the entire Local.

After nine weeks of attack and counterattack, a court case against the pickets, which was finally thrown out, and great Company and Union losses, a settlement was reached. The Company finally agreed to the rewording of the contract, and granted another paid holiday, and the radio carried news flashes to the workers. A mass meeting was called for the following day--the new contract was read, questions answered, and a vote taken. An overwhelming majority voted to end the strike, and a victory parade formed. A representative went across the street, signed the new contract, and came back waving the small book as a symbol of victory. The following day work was resumed at Selbys.

In conclusion, I have tried to point out those

aspects of the strike and its background that determined the end it had. I feel very strongly that the key to the Union's success was the recognition and use of certain sociological principles of group behavior. We find underlying every policy and incident in the strike an awareness of these principles, and reflected in the headlines, and devices, etc., a clear understanding of how these principles can be played upon.

Appendix 3: A Partial Family Genealogy

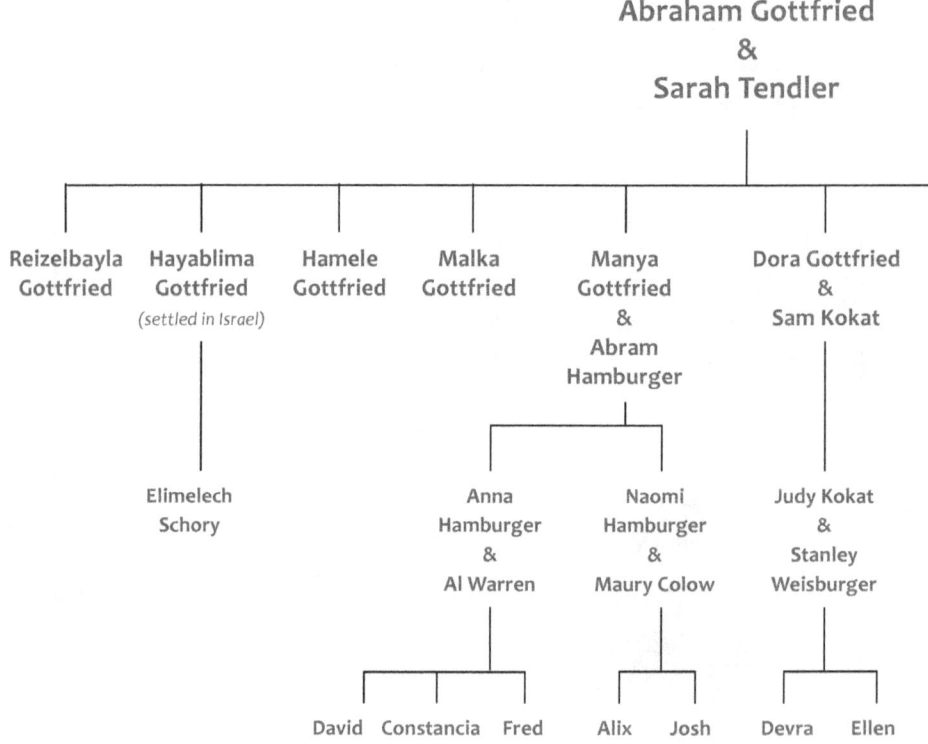

Appendix 3: Genealogy | 83

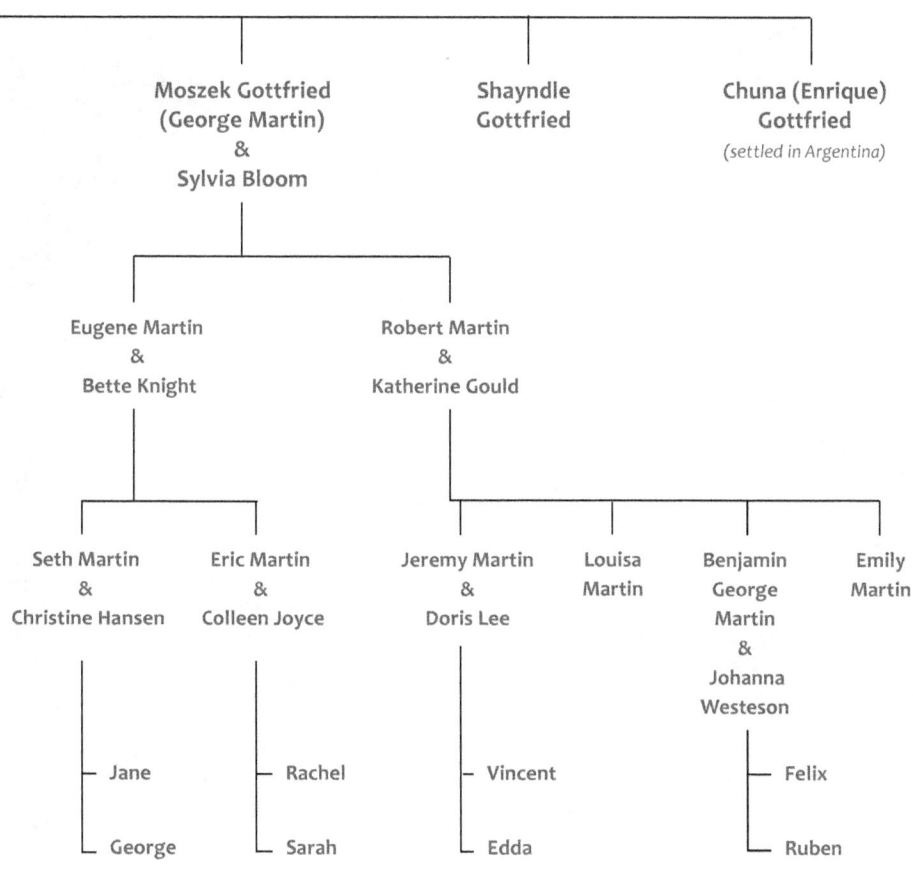

Appendix 4: A Retrospective on the "Communist-Dominated" Unions

I described earlier how the wave of anti-Communism after World War II swept through the labor movement. After a prolonged internal struggle within the national leadership of the CIO, the right-wing forces led by Walter Reuther launched a campaign to purge Communists and Communist sympathizers from the locals and expelled entire locals that were viewed as "Communist-dominated." George Martin was in all likelihood not a Communist, but as an avowed leftist and progressive he was sympathetic to many aspects of the Communist movement. In any case, he was without doubt on the list of those to be purged, and, as we saw, he was eventually forced out of the CIO.

The Shoe Workers was one of the 18 branches of the CIO that were labeled "Communist-dominated" by Congressional aide Max Kampelman in a 1950 paper.[6] Kampelman, who helped to orchestrate the purge of Communists from the CIO, based his classification on political issues raised, causes advocated, and positions taken—mostly on foreign policy. Eventually eleven of these branches were expelled. Interestingly, the United Shoe Workers of America was not one of them; this was explained in a book called *Left Out: Reds and America's Industrial Unions*, by sociologists Judith Stepan-Norris and Maurice Zeitlin (Cambridge Press, 2002), in a passage that applies directly to George Martin:

---

6. Kampelman, Max M. 1957. *The Communist Party vs. the CIO*. NewYork: Prager. Reprint, New York: Arno and the *New York Times*, 1971.

> The "rank-and-file uprisings" that they [the right-wing leadership of the CIO] expected and did all they could to engender never came. They could not "dislodge" the Communists from power. In four other internationals in the Communist camp (maritime (NMU), transport (TWU), the Furniture Workers, and the Shoe Workers), the Communists were "dislodged" only when their presidents, and some other top officers, taking care to continue to identify themselves as men of the left, reneged in time to prevent their union's expulsion; they denounced and turned against their erstwhile Communist comrades and succeeded in ousting them from office. (p. 273)

The anti-Communist forces within the CIO claimed that they were saving the trade union movement from harm. They often argued that the Communist-dominated unions subordinated the needs of the workers to those of the Soviet regime, that these unions settled for unfavorable contracts, and that they were undemocratic in their internal affairs. Stepan-Norris and Zeitlin found exactly the opposite:

> We find that in all four periods on almost every provision examined, the local contracts won by Communist-led unions were far more likely to be pro-labor than those won by the unions in the "shifting" and anti-Communist camps. In fact, most of the contracts won by locals of Communist-led internationals were pro-labor on almost every provision in every period. This was so even during World War II, when the CP advocated "class collaboration," and even in the late postwar period, when the Communist-led unions were besieged by enemies on all sides.

They continued:

> But these findings on World War II, which are contrary to the nearly monolithic consensus among writers spanning the political spectrum, must surely leave many readers incredulous. The simple historical fact revealed here is that—whatever the demands

of the antifascist war effort and the rhetorical extremes of CP officials—the wartime contracts won by the Communist-led unions were far less likely than those of their rivals on the right to cede "management prerogatives," to sign away the "right" to strike, or to have cumbersome grievance procedures: 65 percent of the wartime agreements won by locals of the Communist-led unions did not cede management prerogatives, and only 27 percent entirely prohibited strikes for the duration of the contract. But, in contrast, 55 percent of the wartime contracts negotiated by locals of the shifting camp and 67 percent in the anti-Communist camp did cede management prerogatives, and 54 and 73 percent, respectively, banned strikes entirely for the contract's term.

Stepan-Norris and Zeitlin concluded that "the CIO's Communist-led unions were among the most egalitarian and progressive on class, race, and gender issues, and fought to enlarge the freedom and enhance the human dignity of America's workers."

www.ingramcontent.com/pod-product-compliance
Lightning Source LLC
Chambersburg PA
CBHW031412040426
42444CB00005B/526